LONDON'S ALX400 BUSES

DAVID BEDDALL

AMBERLEY

First published 2021

Amberley Publishing
The Hill, Stroud
Gloucestershire, GL5 4EP

www.amberley-books.com

Copyright © David Beddall, 2021

The right of David Beddall to be identified as
the Author of this work has been asserted in
accordance with the Copyrights, Designs and
Patents Act 1988.

ISBN 978 1 3981 0630 7 (print)
ISBN 978 1 3981 0631 4 (ebook)

British Library Cataloguing in Publication Data.
A catalogue record for this book is available from
the British Library.

Origination by Amberley Publishing.
Printed in the UK.

Introduction

The Alexander ALX400 was the first low-floor double-deck body to be produced for the UK bus industry, first appearing in 1997. It was part of a range of vehicles produced by Alexander (ALX100 to ALX500), with all but the ALX100 featuring a similar design at the front and rear of the vehicle. The ALX400 was built to replace the Alexander R-series double-deck bodies. It was first available on the DAF DB250LF chassis, which just beat Dennis with the Trident model as being the first low-floor double-decker in the UK. A third chassis was offered in 2000, when Volvo introduced the B7TL model. The ALX400 was a big hit in London, with all the major operators taking stock of the type, operating all three of the previously mentioned chassis in the capital. It was also popular outside of London, with large volume orders being placed by Stagecoach, with First Group and Arriva also taking examples of the type into stock. Independent operators also took stock of new models of the ALX400, as well as taking advantage of cascades from the larger groups when they arose. Dublin Bus also became a fan of the type, taking 658 over a six-year period.

The Alexander ALX400-bodied DAF DB250LF was the first combination to enter service in London in the latter part of 1998, entering service with Arriva London from Wood Green. The DB250LF was a modified version of the original DB250 model which had first been introduced to the UK in 1991, and into London service in 1992. The first DB250LF was bodied by Optare on the Spectra model, and was also offered on other body styles after the ALX400 had been introduced. Arriva London took a large quantity of the DB250LF/ALX400 combination, with a small batch also being ordered by Arriva The Shires for a couple of north London contracts.

The Dennis Trident/Alexander ALX400 combination first appeared in 1999, with Stagecoach London being the first operator to take stock of the type. The Tridents with Stagecoach were built to a lower height, and also featured a staircase behind the driver, rather than the straight centre staircase preferred by London Regional Transport. Stagecoach had done this with the thought of cascading these vehicles to its provincial operators in years to come. The Trident/ALX400 combination became the most popular choice among London operators, with Metroline, First London and Connex London also taking volume orders of the type.

The third offering was from Volvo with the B7TL model, first introduced in 1999. Like its predecessor, the Olympian, the B7TL also became popular with a number of operators, and was again available on other body styles which were also purchased by London operators. Go-Ahead London took a small number of the type, with First London and Arriva London placing volume orders for the type.

Transbus International was formed in 2001, amalgamating Dennis, Plaxton and Alexander, with the model becoming known as the Transbus ALX400 after this point. However, the Mayflower Group, owner of Transbus International, got into financial difficulty in 2004, with a new company being formed, under the name of Alexander Dennis Limited (ADL) in 2005.

Late 2005 saw the introduction of the ADL Enviro 400 double-deck body, which saw the beginning of the end for the production of the ALX400 model. In 2006 it was decided to discontinue the ALX400 model, with the last of the type entering service with Stagecoach

London. The ALX400 remained in London service until 2019, with some of the type hanging on in London as driver training and private hire vehicles.

The ALX400 had a number of rivals over the years, the original one being the Plaxton President that launched around the same time. East Lancs introduced the Vyking and Myllennium models which also saw large competition for the ALX400. Wrightbus of Ballymena produced their first double-deck bus body in 2000, known as the Eclipse Gemini. The introduction of this new model saw large orders for the type placed by London operators, who seemed to be impressed by this new, but more expensive, model.

Despite the competition from the other bus body builders mentioned above, Alexander and its subsequent incarnations, a total of 2,194 ALX400 models were supplied to London bus operators between 1999 and 2006.

This book is split into three parts, starting with a look at the DAF DB250LFs, followed by a section depicting ALX400-bodied Dennis Tridents, concluding with a section devoted to the Volvo B7TLs that carried ALX400 bodywork.

David Beddall
Rushden, 2020

Arriva London received the first low-floor double-decker, in the form of an Alexander ALX400-bodied DAF DB250LF registered R101GNW. It was delivered in May 1998 to Wood Green garage, before returning to Alexander's factory in Falkirk for certification. After being replaced by newer rolling stock in June 2008, DLA1 joined other members of the class in the driver training fleet. For this, it wore a special aquamarine livery as seen in the photograph above. In May 2018 it was restored to its original livery, and was sold to the Bromley Bus Preservation Group in January 2020. It is seen attending the RM60 celebrations in Finsbury Park in 2014. (Liam Farrer-Beddall)

The first batch of twenty DLAs were delivered to Clapton in October and November 1998 for use on the 242. Eleven of this batch transferred to Wood Green in April 2006 for further work. DLA18 (S218JUA) was one of those originally allocated to Clapton, moving to Wood Green as mentioned. It is seen on layover at Edgware bus station blinded for its return journey to Turnpike Lane station on route 221. (David Beddall)

DLA21 (S221JUA) was the last of the twenty originally allocated to Clapton garage in the autumn of 1998. After transfer to Wood Green in April 2006, it was reallocated to the training school at Edmonton in June 2008. It is seen wearing full training livery, passing Edmonton Green bus station, followed by a Wright Eclipse Gemini-bodied Volvo B7TL. (Liam Farrer-Beddall)

Arriva London South received their first DLAs in January 1999 when seventeen such vehicles were allocated to Thornton Heath garage to take up service on the 250 (Brixton–Croydon Town Centre). DLA49 (S249JUA) represents this batch, and is captured by the camera on the forecourt of Thornton Heath garage, blinded for route 289. (David Beddall)

Wood Green received another twenty-nine of the type in the spring of 1999 for routes 102 and 329. In January 2006 the batch were reallocated to both Enfield and Barking garages. DLA81 (S281JUA) was one of those transferred to Enfield. It is seen entering Edmonton Green bus station. (Liam Farrer-Beddall)

DLA90 (S290JUA) is another of the batch originally delivered to Wood Green in the spring of 1999. It is seen on layover at Walthamstow while operating a rail replacement service. The central staircase can be seen clearly in this view. (David Beddall)

DLA95 (T295FGN) is captured by the camera passing Edmonton Green bus station on the lengthy service 279 (Manor House–Waltham Cross). It is seen bound for Manor House wearing the all-red livery. It was one of three DLAs delivered to Wood Green in May 1999, passing to Enfield in November 2002. (Liam Farrer-Beddall)

The summer of 1999 saw nineteen Alexander ALX400-bodied DAF DB250LFs arrive at Stamford Hill, primarily for the 188, numbered DLA97 to DLA115. They were also used on other routes from the depot including the 254 (Holloway–Aldgate Station). DLA109 (T309FGN) is seen loading at Hackney Central while operating the latter service. It shows the original Arriva 'Cow Horn' livery well. (Liam Farrer-Beddall)

DLA151 (V351DGT) was one of twelve DLAs allocated to Brixton garage in November 1999 for route 59 (Streatham Hill–Kings Cross). March 2010 saw DLA151 transfer to Enfield, and here it is seen at Waltham Cross having operated a journey on the 317. (Liam Farrer-Beddall)

In the early 2000s, a number of London Buses were decorated in overall advertisements for West End musicals. DLA166 (W366VGJ) was one such vehicle, and was painted black to advertise *Chicago*. Part of a batch delivered new to Norwood for use on the 68, it is seen passing through Streatham Hill on route 249 towards Anerley station. (David Beddall)

DLA173 (W373WGJ) was another of the batch originally allocated to Norwood for route 68. It too is seen off route, operating a journey on the 417, reaching journey's end at Crystal Palace. (Liam Farrer-Beddall)

Another view of the Arriva turquoise driver training livery, taken at Edmonton Green. DLA175 (W375WGJ) was new to Norwood for route 68, moving to Croydon in September 2003 and Beddington Farm in September 2012. Three months later it became a driver training vehicle from this depot, before transferring north of the river in early 2013. (Liam Farrer-Beddall)

DLA190 (W434WGJ) arrived at Wood Green in June 2000 for use on the W3. It is seen carrying Enfield garage codes while passing through the Turnpike Lane area, bound for Tottenham Hale on route 41. (Liam Farrer-Beddall)

DLA192 (W392WGJ) was another June 2000 delivery to Wood Green garage, moving to Enfield in August 2002. It is seen in full Arriva London livery departing Waltham Cross bus station, about to embark on its lengthy journey to Manor House. (Liam Farrer-Beddall)

Clapham Junction provides the backdrop for this photograph of DLA205 (W436WGJ). New to Tottenham in August 2000, it transferred to Brixton in April 2004. It is from this garage that route 319 operates. It is seen heading for its home garage, which on route destinations is known as Streatham Hill, Telford Avenue. (Liam Farrer-Beddall)

Arriva London South's Croydon garage took stock of nine DLA class ALX400s in October 2000, followed by six more in December. DLA223 (X423FGP) was one of those delivered during October. Originally intended to operate the 468, it is seen crossing the tramlines on the edge of Croydon town centre while heading towards Purley, operating a journey on the 412. (Liam Farrer-Beddall)

DLA240 (X503GGO) is overshadowed by the bridges that carry the rail lines through the Waterloo area. It was new to Tottenham in February 2001 for route 243 (Wood Green–Waterloo). A VLW class Wright Eclipse Gemini-bodied Volvo B7TL can be seen parked behind DLA240. It is this type that saw the demise of the DLA class at Wood Green garage. (David Beddall)

DLA256 (X508GGO) was allocated to Croydon in February 2001, remaining there until 2013. It is pictured at West Croydon station, blinded for route 412 to Purley. (David Beddall)

Hyde Park Corner finds DLA271 (Y471UGC) heading towards Streatham Hill on route 137. The 137 is now in the hands of LT class New Bus for London double-decks. (Liam Farrer-Beddall)

DLA290 (Y523UGC) was a much-travelled vehicle, operating for a number of Arriva London garages, both north and south of the river. New to Tottenham garage in June 2001, it was reallocated to Edmonton and Stamford Hill, before entering service at Brixton in August 2005. It is seen leaving Victoria, with Victoria station dominating the background, while heading to Hyde Park Corner on a short working of route 2. (Liam Farrer-Beddall)

Croydon town centre finds DLA314 (Y514UGC) almost completing its journey from Brixton on route 109. It was new to Norwood in June 2001 and transferred to Brixton in September 2006. It is from the latter garage that the 109 is operated. (Liam Farrer-Beddall)

DLA335 (LG52DCY), one of twenty-six such vehicles allocated to Thornton Heath over the course of February and March 2003. It is seen out of service before setting out on the 289. (David Beddall)

DLA371 (LJ03MVC) leads a line-up of five double-deckers, passing through Brixton. The ALX400 was one of the first generation of low-floor double-deckers, the rest of the line-up consisting of the second-generation low-floor models, the Wrightbus Eclipse Gemini 2 and a trio of Enviro 400s. It is seen starting its journey on the 109 to Croydon town centre. (Liam Farrer-Beddall)

The final batch of DLAs were delivered to Clapton garage to replace Alexander-bodied Leyland Olympians on route 253 (Hackney Central–Euston). In April 2006 the batch transferred to Stamford Hill after the closure of Clapton garage. DLA383 (LJ03MUB) represents this batch, after its transfer to Thornton Heath in February 2010. (Liam Farrer-Beddall)

December 2002 saw the arrival of twenty-five Alexander ALX400-bodied DAF DB250LFs with Arriva The Shires & Essex at Garston garage. Delivered in the standard Arriva London livery, they entered service on routes 142 (Watford Junction–Brent Cross) and 340 (Edgware Station–Harrow Bus Station). 6011 (KL52CXC) is seen on layover at Edgware bus station while operating the latter service. (David Beddall)

6016 (KL52CXH) is seen wearing the revised all-red livery, relieved by a yellow band. It is seen exiting Brent Cross Shopping Centre, beginning its journey to Watford Junction on service 142. (Liam Farrer-Beddall)

An increase on the TfL contracts in North London led Arriva The Shires & Essex to purchase an additional ALX400-bodied VDL DB250 double-deck. 6025 (YJ54CFG) is seen on layover at Edgware bus station before returning to Harrow on the 340. (Liam Farrer-Beddall)

April 2006 saw the transfer of thirteen Alexander ALX400-bodied DAF DB250LFs to Arriva Southern Counties at Dartford. They were put to further use on London contracts, retaining the London red livery. 6230 (Y463UGC) was one of those transferred, and is seen entering Bexleyheath town centre while operating a journey on the 492 towards Sidcup station. (Liam Farrer-Beddall)

Stagecoach London's Leyton garage was the first to operate the Dennis Trident model on routes 48, 55 and 56. Thirty-eight of the type initially entered service in January 1999, being followed by TA1 (S801BWC), which had arrived in Stagecoach's stripped livery. TA1, numbered 17001 in January 2003, is seen operating a private hire contract while negotiating Trafalgar Square. (Liam Farrer-Beddall)

Stratford bus station finds 17047 (T647KPU), originally numbered TA47. It is seen wearing the 2001 Stagecoach corporate livery. The giant Olympic countdown clock can be seen in the background. (David Beddall)

Further Tridents soon followed for other garages, including Barking. In June 2006, the London operations of Stagecoach were sold to Australian banking group Macquarie Bank. Under their new owner, vehicles were adorned with East London and Selkent fleet names. This is demonstrated by 17065 (T665KPU), seen at Romford station wearing the new East London fleet names. (David Beddall)

Another shot taken at Stratford bus station. 17095 (T695KPU) is seen loading before setting off to Beckton on route 262. The line-up of single-deckers on the left of the picture shows the variety of types that once graced Stratford. (David Beddall)

Barking garage finds 17104 and 17105 (V104/5MEV) – both withdrawn from mainstream London service – being used as driver training vehicles. Both vehicles were converted to this use in July 2009 after being withdrawn from London service the month before. (Liam Farrer-Beddall)

17114 (V114MEV) was new to Plumstead garage in November 1999, and was used on routes 53, 96, 99, 122 and 177. Less than a year later, in September 2000, it moved to North Street, Romford garage for further service. It is photographed loading at Romford station, bound for Dagenham on route 174. (Liam Farrer-Beddall)

17149 (V149MEV) was one of eleven ALX400-bodied Tridents delivered to Catford in December 1999. They were originally put to use on the 54 and 136. Under the control of the East London Bus Group, 17149 transferred to Bow. It is seen travelling to the stand at Marble Arch, having travelled in from Hackney Wick on route 30. (Liam Farrer-Beddall)

New to Bow garage in December 1999 for use on the 26 (Waterloo–Hackney Wick) was 17161 (V161MEV). The following year it transferred to Plumstead, where it remained until being withdrawn in 2011. It is seen loading in Woolwich, in an area now pedestrianised, showing the Selkent fleet names applied to vehicles based at Catford, Bromley and Plumstead under the control of the East London Bus Group. (David Beddall)

Stratford also received a batch of ALX400-bodied Tridents in December 1999. 17186 (V186MEV) was the first of twelve such vehicles to be received, originally numbered TA186 by Stagecoach. Like many Tridents in the fleet, 17186 moved around various garages. In March 2007, it was allocated to Barking where it stayed until withdrawal in 2011. The Docklands Light Railway station at Canning Town provides the backdrop to this photograph. (Liam Farrer-Beddall)

17187 (V362OWC) was another Dennis Trident to be delivered to Stagecoach in December 1999, and was part of a batch of fifteen to enter service from Leyton on route 48, replacing Volvo Olympians on this route. It moved to Barking in August 2009, from which garage route 5 (Romford Market–Canning Town) operates. It is seen departing the Romford station stop. (Liam Farrer-Beddall)

In December 2001 Plumstead garage received TA193 (V193MEV) from Leyton. In January 2003, TA193 was renumbered 17193 in Stagecoach's national numbering sequence. It is seen here under the ownership of the East London Bus Group, paused at Thamesmead before returning to North Greenwich via Woolwich on route 472. (Liam Farrer-Beddall)

August and September 2000 saw the arrival of a batch of shorter 9.9-metre Dennis Tridents. 17223 (X361NNO) was the first of these to be delivered, being allocated to Catford replacing Volvo Olympians. The class code TAS was allocated to these shorter vehicles. It moved to East London at North Street, Romford in February 2006, from where it operated until July 2009, at which point it was reallocated to Barking. It is seen picking up passengers at Romford station. (Liam Farrer-Beddall)

The winter of 2000/2001 saw longer 10.5-metre Tridents taken into stock at Plumstead, which replaced a number of Northern Counties-bodied Volvo Olympians, which in turn went to other Stagecoach London garages to replace Leyland Titans. 17268 (X268NNO) was one such vehicle, originally numbered TA268. It is seen heading towards Thamesmead on the 472, photographed at Woolwich town centre. (Liam Farrer-Beddall)

At the same time, a small batch of similar length Tridents were delivered to Leyton. They were short-lived at this garage, moving to Bromley in September 2001. 17282 (X282NNO) is seen at Lewisham station, having completed a journey from Orpington. (Liam Farrer-Beddall)

17297 (X297NNO) is photographed in the Aldwych, a short journey away from its final destination south of the river at Waterloo. Stagecoach London lost the 26 (Hackney Wick–Waterloo) to Tower Transit in 2011. (Liam Farrer-Beddall)

January 2001 saw the arrival of fifteen ALX400-bodied Tridents at Plumstead. The majority of the batch remained true to Plumstead throughout their London service. Originally numbered TA304, X304NNO was renumbered 17304 in January 2003. It is seen at the Bexleyheath terminus of route 99, having travelled in from Woolwich. (David Beddall)

A further twenty-five similar vehicles were delivered to Bromley in February 2001. Unlike the Plumstead batch delivered the month before, a number of these vehicles transferred to other Stagecoach London garages. However, 17352 (X352NNO) remained true to Bromley until withdrawal in 2012. It is seen heading to Lewisham, in Bromley. (Liam Farrer-Beddall)

17368 (Y368NHK) stands in the pouring rain at Catford garage. New to Barking in June 2001, it was converted to a driver training vehicle in March 2013. The livery of the time chosen for the training fleet was the 2001 London corporate livery, the main fleet by this time being painted 100 per cent red. (Liam Farrer-Beddall)

17373 (Y373NHK) was another of the thirty-two-strong fleet of ALX400-bodied Tridents delivered to Barking between June and September 2001. It remained at Barking until 2011 when it transferred to Catford. It is seen passing Barking garage, with an Optare Versa and a Dennis Dart SLF being visible in the yard. (Liam Farrer-Beddall)

Photographed parked in the open-air parking ground at Barking garage is 17383 (LX51FPF), while under the ownership of the East London Bus Group. The blue and orange swoops of its former owner can be seen at the rear of the vehicle. (Liam Farrer-Beddall)

A wet North Street garage in Romford provides the backdrop to this photograph of 17393 (Y393NHK). 17393 was new as TA393 to Stratford. It transferred to Romford in 2011. (Liam Farrer-Beddall)

17396 (LX51FHO) provides another view of the driver training livery worn by a number of Alexander ALX400-bodied Dennis Tridents designated to this role. 17396 was new to Stratford, moving to West Ham when Stratford was closed for redevelopment into the Olympic Park. It was converted to a driver training vehicle in June 2010, remaining at West Ham. It is seen passing Newham Town Hall, East Ham. (Liam Farrer-Beddall)

17401 (Y401NHK) was new to Stratford in July 2001. It operated with Stagecoach until 2013, when it was withdrawn. It is seen on layover at Marble Arch before heading back to Hackney Wick on route 30. A similar-bodied Volvo B7TL VLA class of Arriva London is seen sneaking past on its way to Marylebone. (Liam Farrer-Beddall)

156 shorter ALX400s were purchased between July 2001 and October 2002. 17447 (Y447NHK) was delivered to Stratford in August 2001. Twenty-two shorter Tridents were transferred to Rainham garage under the control of East London in July 2009. Vehicles operating from this garage gained Thameside fleet names as shown above. (Liam Farrer-Beddall)

17487 (LX51FME) is captured by the camera paused on Victoria Dock Road while heading towards Canning Town on route 147. This Trident was new to Bow in October 2001. (Liam Farrer-Beddall)

Twenty-one shorter Tridents were allocated to Stratford in the autumn of 2001 for use on the 106 (Whitechapel–Finsbury Park Station). The later location finds 17506 (LX51FNJ), wearing the new Stagecoach London livery introduced in 2001. The letter 's' was applied after the fleet number post-2003 to denote that these were short vehicles. (David Beddall)

17522 (LX51FOC) is the final member of the batch allocated to Stratford for the 106. New in November 2001, it is seen entering Finsbury Park station wearing full Stagecoach livery. When new it was placed into an all-over advertisement for New York Sightseeing, trying to encourage tourists back to New York after the 9/11 terrorist attacks. (David Beddall)

LY02OAZ was new to Stratford garage in June 2002 as TAS549. It became 17549 in the 2003 Stagecoach renumbering. In April 2006, it was reallocated to Upton Park garage. It is seen heading towards Stratford on the 238, at East Ham. (Liam Farrer-Beddall)

17555 (LY02OBG) arrived a month later at Stratford, entering service in July 2002. Like 17594, it too was transferred to Upton Park in April 2006. The 's' can be seen clearly after the main fleet number. It is photographed at the Hainault Road layover bays in Ilford. (Liam Farrer-Beddall)

Leyton took stock of twenty-three longer ALX400-bodied Tridents in December 2002. Former TA601 (LV52HHL) is seen parked at the exit to Leyton garage, blinded for the 69 to Canning Town. It is seen carrying its 2003 fleet number, 17601. This batch lasted until the first couple of months of 2010 with East London Bus Group before being sold. (David Beddall)

Marble Arch finds a pair of ALX400-bodied Tridents held at a red light. East London's 17741 (LY52ZDZ) has reached journey's end, and is seen blinded for its return journey to Hackney Wick. London United's TLA3 (SN53EUJ) is seen heading towards Acton Green, having started at Piccadilly Circus. (Liam Farrer-Beddall)

17743 (LY52ZFB) was new to Stagecoach London in December 2002, numbered TA653. It is seen on layover at Aldgate bus station, before operating a journey to Paddington Basin on route 15. (David Beddall)

2012 saw a large number of London buses gain all-over advertisements, many of which were used on routes around the Stratford area. 17748 (LY52ZFG) was one of many to gain an advertisement for Vodafone. 17748 was often used on the 86 (Romford Station–Stratford), but when photographed it is seen operating route 175 to Dagenham. It is about to pass under the rail bridge in a wet Romford. (Liam Farrer-Beddall)

The application of all-over advertisements became popular during the 2010s, with a number of London buses gaining such liveries. Most were typically applied to vehicles used on routes into Central London, but some were also applied to vehicles used on routes in the outer suburbs. Romford-based 17759 (LX03BUH) was one such vehicle, gaining an all-over advertisement for Home Sense in 2015. It is seen wearing this livery as it passes Romford station. (Liam Farrer-Beddall)

Nothing but ALX400-bodied Tridents can be seen in this view taken at the former Stratford garage. 17763 (LX03BUV) and 17509 (LX51FNW) are the two closest to the camera. No fewer than 208 ALX400- bodied Tridents were taken into stock by Stagecoach London during 2003, most for general fleet renewal. (David Beddall)

17797 (LX03BWL) was one of forty-seven new ALX400s allocated to Leyton garage in March and April 2003. They were purchased to replace the original batch of low-height ALX400-bodied Tridents operating from Leyton. It is seen on layover in Wood Green, before returning to Upper Walthamstow on route 230. (Liam Farrer-Beddall)

17799 (LX03BWN) is captured by the camera at Stratford bus station operating route 330 to Wanstead Park. It is another of the forty-seven-strong fleet of Tridents delivered to Leyton in March and April 2003. (Liam Farrer-Beddall)

The 10.5-metre ALX400s can be distinguished by the small window located behind the centre exit doors. This can be clearly seen on 17811 (LX03BXF), which is seen at the Yardley Lane Estate terminus of route 215. The 215 runs between the estate and Walthamstow Central. 17811 was captured on its last day in service, 19 August 2019. (Aethan Blake)

17818 (LX03BXN) was one of the April 2003 deliveries to Leyton garage. It transferred to Bow in February 2008, returning to Leyton in June 2009, only to be sent again to Bow in August 2009. It is seen entering Trafalgar Square on the last leg of its journey to Regent Street. (Liam Farrer-Beddall)

June 2003 saw a small batch of Tridents arrive at Barking garage to update the rolling stock used on route 5. 17856 (LX03NEY) was the second member of this batch. It moved to Rainham in October 2008, before returning to Barking the same month. In December 2014 this vehicle moved again, this time to West Ham where it operated until withdrawal in October 2018. It is photographed on Glading Road, Manor Park operating route 104. (Aethan Blake)

Another example of the batch allocated to Barking in June 2003 is 17863 (LX03NFM), which is photographed in Barking town centre. It is seen wearing full Stagecoach London livery, complete with East London Bus Group fleet names. (David Beddall)

Sister vehicle 17864 (LX03NFJ) transferred to Bromley in March 2012. It is seen heading towards Bromley North on route 61, passing through the rural-looking Chislehurst Common. By the time this photograph was taken, the 61 was normally operated by Enviro 400s. (Aethan Blake)

17885 (LX03OPT) represents a batch of ten ALX400s allocated to Bow garage in August 2003 to complete the conversion of route 15 to low-floor buses from Routemaster operation. In August 2010 it transferred to Barking. 17885 is photographed on Valence Avenue, Becontree heading towards Barking on the 62. (Aethan Blake)

17899 (LX03ORP) is seen at rest inside Barking garage. This photograph shows the popularity of the ALX range with Stagecoach, with another ALX400 on the left of 17899, and half of an ALX200-bodied Dennis Dart SLF saloon on the right of the photograph. (Liam Farrer-Beddall)

17944 (LX53JYG) was new to Stagecoach London in December 2003. Originally allocated to Plumstead, it moved to West Ham garage in September 2011 after operating at Bow and Upton Park. It is seen at Stratford Broadway in 2012, the railings adorned with London 2012 banners. (Liam Farrer-Beddall)

North Street, Romford's allocation of vehicles tends to stick to the north-east London area. Therefore, 17978 (LX53KAE) seems a little lost as it passes St Pancras International while operating route 205 despite displaying full route branding for route 247 (Barkingside Park–Romford Station). A burst water main in Bow Road preventing access to Bow garage led to this unusual working. (Liam Farrer-Beddall)

17983 (LX53KBE) is seen in the correct operating area for route 247, starting its journey at Romford station heading towards Barkingside. Route branding was applied to all routes operating through the Barkingside area of East London in 2017. The Stagecoach London Tridents were not the only ALX400s to adorn route branding under this scheme, with a further example being shown later in this book. (Liam Farrer-Beddall)

Romford received twenty-four shorter 9.9-metre-long ALX400-bodied Tridents during January and February 2004. They were put to use on the 247 (Romford–Collier Row–Hainault–Barkingside). Representing the batch is 17997 (LX53KCG), seen passing Romford station. (David Beddall)

17999 (LX04GCU) was the last of the twenty-four short Tridents allocated to North Street, Romford early in 2004. It remained allocated there until August 2016 when it transferred to Barking. It is photographed passing through Barking town centre on route 169, shortly before terminating. (Liam Farrer-Beddall)

By the time Stagecoach London received its next batch of ALX400s, around 200 of the type had been allocated to provincial operations around the UK. Therefore, the next batch were numbered from 18201 onwards. Thirty-eight arrived in March to replace Routemasters on the 8 (Bow Church–Victoria Station). 18210 (LX04FWW) is pictured at the Waterden Road, Stratford open day in 2005 sporting an all-over advertisement for 'Back the Bid', for London to host the 2012 Olympic Games. (David Beddall)

18212 (LX04FWZ) is another of the batch purchased to convert route 8 to low-floor buses. In December 2014, it transferred to West Ham garage. It is seen heading towards Stratford on route 473, paused at the North Woolwich stop. (Aethan Blake)

Another of Bow's allocation for route 8 is 18214 (LX04FXB), seen broken down at Victoria, the rear of the tow truck just visible. The Victoria Palace Theatre can also be seen in the background of this photograph. (David Beddall)

The introduction of the New Bus for London on the 8 saw the cascade of the Tridents to other garages. 18215 (LX04FYC) moved to Bromley in September 2014. It is seen in Bexleyheath starting its journey to Bromley North on route 269. (Liam Farrer-Beddall)

The batch did stray on to other services operating from Bow. 18224 (LX04FXM) shows this, operating route 30. It is photographed on layover at Marble Arch. (Liam Farrer-Beddall)

18242 (LX04FYJ) was one of eighteen ALX400-bodied Tridents allocated to Leyton garage for the conversion of route 230 (Wood Green–Upper Walthamstow) to double-deck. It is seen operating a journey on the 115 when transferred to West Ham in November 2009. (Liam Farrer-Beddall)

18268 (LX05BWA) was new to Stagecoach London at Stratford in February 2005, lasting with the company until March 2019. In 2011 it was transferred to West Ham where it remained until withdrawal. It is photographed at Canning Town bus station, heading to its stand while operating route 330. (Liam Farrer-Beddall)

Twelve ALX400s arrived at Stratford in February 2005 to take over the 158 (Chingford Mount–Stratford) from First London. 18270 (LX05BWC) represents the batch, parked at Stratford bus station wearing the 100 per cent red livery. (Liam Farrer-Beddall)

Another of this batch is seen departing Walthamstow Central bound for Wood Green on route 230. The vehicle viewed here is 18272 (LX05BWE). In the background, a Wright Eclipse Gemini can be seen. This was one of the rivals of the ALX400, with Arriva London taking a large number of this type. (Liam Farrer-Beddall)

18455 (LX55EPA) was new to North Street, Romford in September 2005. In 2009, it moved south of the river to Catford, where it operated for ten years before withdrawal. It is seen negotiating the remodelled Elephant & Castle roundabout while operating a journey on the 136. (Liam Farrer-Beddall)

18466 (LX55EPU) was one of eighteen allocated to Stratford for route 257. It is seen straying off its intended route, operating the 238. Stratford Broadway provides the background for this photograph. (Liam Farrer-Beddall)

Eighteen ALX400s were allocated to Stratford garage in October 2005 to operate the 257 (Walthamstow Central–Stratford). In October 2012, the batch moved to Romford for further use. 18479 (LX55ESN) is seen operating from the latter garage on route 247, photographed at Romford station. (Liam Farrer-Beddall)

New to Stagecoach London in February 2006 was 18487 (LX55BFF). It was originally used on the 47, before being transferred to Bromley in 2016. Two years later, in April 2018, it joined West Ham's allocation for a few months before withdrawal. It is seen at East Beckton Sainsbury's on route 262. (Aethan Blake)

Catford's route 47 took stock of the last ALX400s with Stagecoach London. 18498 (LX06AHE) is seen here out of service, with Catford garage providing the background. (David Beddall)

Numerically, 18499 (LX06AHF) was the last ALX400-bodied Trident to be taken into stock by a London operator. It is seen passing Lewisham police station while heading to Shoreditch on route 47. It is closely followed by a Go-Ahead London Plaxton President. (Liam Farrer-Beddall)

A shortage of ALX400-bodied Tridents in October 2008 led to the loan of nine 9.9-metre versions from Metroline to the Selkent division of the East London Bus Group. They gained temporary five-digit fleet numbers. 18887 (T68KLD) was one of those loaned to Selkent. It is seen operating from Bromley garage, photographed at Bexleyheath town centre before travelling back to Bromley North. (David Beddall)

Stagecoach London entered the London sightseeing tour market in 2018, with nine ALX400s being converted to either partial open-top or fully open-topped layout. In March 2018 they also gained a blue-based livery, and the tour was branded as 'Megasightseeing.com'. 18467 (LX55EPV) is seen at Elephant and Castle on the London Eye Tour. The Tridents were also given names; 18467 was known as *King George V*. (Liam Farrer-Beddall)

18474 (LX55ERV) was rebuilt to full open-top layout. It is seen passing Marble Arch, and was named *Queen Victoria*. The smart 'Megasightseeing' livery can be clearly seen in this view. The ALX400s remained on the service for the 2018 season, being replaced by Enviro 400s in 2019. They were transferred out of London, with some passing to Stagecoach Midlands for sightseeing work in Stratford-upon-Avon during the year. (Liam Farrer-Beddall)

Although Metroline purchased a large quantity of Plaxton Presidents on both the Dennis Trident and Volvo B7TL chassis, the company also purchased ninety-one Alexander ALX400-bodied Dennis Tridents between 1999 and 2005. The first were delivered to Cricklewood in June and July 1999 and used on the 16 between Cricklewood and Victoria. TA69 (T69KLD) was one of this batch, and is seen on layover at Brent Cross after working the 266 from Hammersmith. (David Beddall)

Another of the original batch of Tridents for the 16 is TA71 (T41KLD). It seen on layover at Tennyson Road, Waterloo while operating route 139. The infamous smart blue and red livery of Metroline is shown off well in this photograph. (David Beddall)

By far the largest batch of ALX400-bodied Tridents purchased by Metroline arrived between August and October 1999, totalling thirty-six. They were initially allocated to Harrow Weald garage for the 140 (Heathrow Airport–Harrow Weald), but were later spread around Metroline's garages. TA88 (T188CLO) joined Cricklewood's allocation in March 2009. It is photographed during a driver changeover. The building to the left of the picture is the new Cricklewood garage. (Liam Farrer-Beddall)

March 2009 also saw Cricklewood gain TA92 (T192CLO), previously operating from Perivale after its stint at Harrow Weald. It is seen parked at Edgware bus station, having operated a journey on the 32 from Kilburn Park. (David Beddall)

TA94 (T194CLO) is seen wearing the original livery applied to the Tridents – note the darker blue skirt than those seen in the previous few photographs. It is seen in the rear yard of Harrow Weald garage, having a break from the 140. (David Beddall)

Numerically the penultimate member of the original batch of Tridents is TA116 (V316GLB). It is seen after its transfer to Cricklewood, at journey's end entering Edgware station on route 32. (Liam Farrer-Beddall)

Seventeen longer ALX400-bodied Tridents arrived at Cricklewood in October 2000 to take up service on the 16, replacing the 1999 delivery of similar vehicles. Given the class code TAL, these vehicles measured 10.5 metres in length, compared to 9.9 metres of the shorter TA class. TAL124 (X324HLL) is seen off route, travelling down Oxford Street while operating the 189 from Brent Cross. (David Beddall)

Route 16 uses the outside parking area of Cricklewood garage as a layover area, an area of the garage that is easily photographed using a longer lens. It is this location that we find TAL129 (X329HLL), blinded for its return trip to Victoria. (Liam Farrer-Beddall)

The final batch of ALX400s taken into stock by Metroline were delivered over the course of April and May 2005. Totalling twenty-two, they were allocated to Cricklewood where they took up service on the 266 (Hammersmith–Brent Cross). TA640 (LK05GFX) is seen leaving Hammersmith, with the infamous Hammersmith Flyover and Hammersmith Apollo in the background. (Liam Farrer-Beddall)

TA647 (LK05GGO) is photographed at the other end of the route, departing Brent Cross bus station. This batch was new in the smaller blue skirt livery. The branch deflectors fitted to the upper near-side front seem moulded to the shape of the bodywork, and did not stick out from the bodywork too much. (Liam Farrer-Beddall)

Metroline lost the contract for the 266 to First London in 2012. The 05-registered ALX400s were then refurbished and repainted before being used on contract services for the London 2012 Olympic Games. TA650 (LK05GGY) shows of its fresh coat of paint as it exits the Eaton Manor Transport hub, located in the Leyton area, located opposite the Olympic Park. (Liam Farrer-Beddall)

The newer 05-registered ALX400-bodied Tridents, originally purchased for use on the 266, were also put to use on other services. TA659 (LK05GHH) is seen operating route 32 towards Kilburn Park, photographed on Kilburn High Road. (Liam Farrer-Beddall)

Connex was the third operator to take stock of the ALX400-bodied Trident combination. 2002 deliveries saw a number enter service on the 156. TA107 (KV02URR) is seen at journey's end at Wimbledon. The Trident and Alexander badges are prominent on the front of this Trident. (David Beddall)

TA111 (KV02URJ) is also seen in Wimbledon, having just completed its journey from Vauxhall. The smart deep-blue skirt and red livery worn by Connex's fleet can be seen clearly in this view. (David Beddall)

First London purchased the ALX400's rival, the Plaxton President, in large quantities over the years. They did, however, purchase sixty-six ALX400-bodied Tridents between 2000 and 2004. The first batch comprised twenty-two of the type for use on the 25. These were delivered in April and May 2000. After the loss of route 25 to Stagecoach East London in 2004, many of these early Tridents moved across to Westbourne Park. Originally numbered TAL936, TNA32936 (W936ULL) is seen operating route 7, heading to Russell Square. (Ian Armstrong)

The winter of 2003 and 2004 saw the arrival of forty-six ALX400-bodied Tridents at Westbourne Park, predominantly for the 23. TNA33356 (LK53EXU), originally numbered TAL1356, is seen at Trafalgar Square operating route 23 toward Westbourne Park Underground station. (David Beddall)

Members of the forty-four-strong TAL class batch delivered to First London's Westbourne Park garage in the winter of 2003/2004 could be found on most of the double-deck routes from that garage. TNA33359 (formerly TAL1359–LK53EXX) is seen at Hyde Park Corner, heading for Maida Hill on route 414, having started its journey at Putney Bridge station. (David Beddall)

TNA33381 (LK53EZA) is another fine example of First London's contingent of ALX400-bodied Tridents purchased in 2003/2004. It is seen off route on route 10, travelling along Oxford Street bound for Hammersmith. It is followed by a similar-bodied Metroline vehicle. This photograph gives a better view of the willow leaf livery used by the company. (David Beddall)

London United first took stock of the ALX400-bodied Trident in September 2000, when three of these vehicles entered service at Hounslow, being used on any service. The second vehicle of the batch, TA202 (X202UMS), is seen loading at the old bus station in Slough, before setting off to Hounslow on route 81. (Liam Farrer-Beddall)

It was over a year before any more of the type entered service with London United. November 2001 saw the arrival of twenty-two Tridents at Fulwell for use on the 131 (Kingston–Tooting Broadway). TA207 (SN51SYF) represents this batch, showing off the distinctive white, red and grey livery of London United. It is seen in between duties at Tooting Broadway. (Liam Farrer-Beddall)

In March 2016, former TA211 (SN51SYO) was placed into London United's private hire division, United Transit based at Twickenham. It is seen wearing the smart silver and red livery, rounding Hyde Park Corner on a private hire contract. (Liam Farrer-Beddall)

Fulwell took stock of a large number of ALX400-bodied Dennis Tridents between 2001 and 2003 for various route contracts. TA217 (SN51SYW) is seen on the forecourt of its home garage. (Liam Farrer-Beddall)

2002 saw Her Majesty Queen Elizabeth II celebrate her Golden Jubilee. Transport for London decorated fifty London Buses in a gold livery to join in with the celebrations, each gaining corporate sponsorship. The 2002 Showbus rally held at the Imperial War Museum at Duxford finds London United's TA225 (SN51SZU) showing off this livery. (Gary Seamarks)

London United operate a handful of routes that serve the Heathrow Airport area. The 222 (Uxbridge–Hounslow) uses the A4 Bath Road on part of the route, but does not enter Heathrow Airport's central area. TA235 (LG02FAU) is photographed stopped on the Bath Road, heading towards Uxbridge. It is seen wearing the new RATP Group logos. (Liam Farrer-Beddall)

Uxbridge station can be seen in the background of this view of TA245 (LG02FBN). It is seen starting its journey back to Hounslow, sporting the RATP Group logos. (Liam Farrer-Beddall)

Route 57 connects Clapham Park with Kingston, Fairfield bus station. It is at this location that we find TA271 (LG02FDJ), still sporting blinds for Kingston. An East Lancs Myllennium Vyking-bodied Volvo B7TL can be seen parked behind. (David Beddall)

The Kingston area of west London became a hotspot for London United's fleet of ALX400-bodied Tridents. TA317 (SN03DZS) is seen about to pass Cromwell Road bus station in Kington, on the first leg of its journey to Tooting Broadway on route 131. (Liam Farrer-Beddall)

Kingston also finds sister vehicle TA318 (SN03DZT), seen wearing an all-over advertisement for U-Switch, which was applied in September 2016. (Liam Farrer-Beddall)

Fairfield bus station, Kingston finds TA328 (SN03EAM) shortly after it was delivered to London United. It is seen blinded for its return journey to Wimbledon. The original London United livery worn by these vehicles can be seen here. (David Beddall)

Thirty-two 10.5-metre-long ALX400-bodied Tridents were taken into stock at Shepherds Bush in December 2003 for use on the 94 (Piccadilly Circus–Acton Green). TLA1 (SN53EUF) is photographed on Park Lane, after operating a short on the 94. (Liam Farrer-Beddall)

TLA24 (SN53KHZ) is seen travelling down Regent Street while heading out to Acton Green. The extra window bay which makes this vehicle longer than the TA class can be clearly seen in this photograph. (Liam Farrer-Beddall)

A busy Marble Arch finds TLA29 (SN53KJX) heading towards Piccadilly Circus. It is seen wearing full London United Livery, complete with Transdev fleet names. (Liam Farrer-Beddall)

December 2002 and January 2003 saw the delivery of twenty-two Transbus Trident/ALX400 vehicles to Armchair, Brentford. They were painted in a red, orange and black livery. They were put to use on the 237 between Shepherds Bush Green and Hounslow Heath. DT1 (KN52NCD) is seen here passing Hounslow bus station wearing this smart livery. Many of the batch became well used by a number of operators in the London area. First they passed to Metroline in November 2004. Abellio purchased a number of these after they were sold by Metroline, with some being sold by Abellio for further use as London sightseeing buses. (David Beddall)

The National Express Group purchased the operations of Connex Bus on 24 February 2004, with the fleet of Tridents transferring to the newly formed Travel London, the second incarnation of this operator. 9701 (V301KGW) is seen on layover at Vauxhall bus station after completing a journey on the 156 from Wimbledon. This bus was originally numbered TA1 with Connex, and the Battersea garage code (QB) can be seen on the side. (David Beddall)

Vauxhall bus station also finds 9708 (V308KGW), again having completed a journey from Wimbledon on the 156. The Travel London logo used was similar to that applied to vehicles in sister company Travel West Midlands, this being shown in this view. (David Beddall)

TA18 (V318KGW) was new to Connex in January 2000 to operate route 3 between Oxford Circus and Crystal Palace. When Connex was acquired by Travel London, the original fleet numbers were retained by the vehicles in the fleet until a renumbering scheme took place in 2006, bringing in four-digit fleet numbers, as has been seen in the previous two photographs. TA18 became 9718 in this new numbering system. (David Beddall)

Another ALX400-bodied Trident-operated route was the 211, running between Waterloo and Hammersmith. TA95 (KV02USM) is photographed at the latter location, still blinded for Hammersmith. Part of the old Connex livery can be seen on the bottom of the front entrance doors. (David Beddall)

9818 (LG52XYP) is seen after the 2006 renumbering scheme. It is captured on layover at Clapham Junction station after operating a journey on the C3. An example of the ALX400's rival, the Plaxton President, can be seen parked behind. (David Beddall)

9725 (V325KGW), originally TA25 with Connex, transferred to Abellio's Byfleet garage in April 2010, gaining the white and red livery. It is seen showing off this livery while parked at Byfleet. (Liam Farrer-Beddall)

In December 2012, a handful of Tridents allocated to Abellio's Byfleet garage were painted into The Green Bus livery for use on contracts in Surrey. This livery can be seen in the background of the previous photograph. The contract later changed to Bus 2, and this is the livery we find 9736 (Y36HWB) wearing. It is approaching East Croydon station while operating a tram replacement service. (Liam Farrer-Beddall)

Trafalgar Square finds 9762 (YN51KVY) travelling towards Crystal Palace on route 3. It is closely followed by Arriva London's similar-bodied Volvo B7TL VLA147, heading to Streatham on route 159. National Express sold Travel London to NedRailways in October 2010. (Liam Farrer-Beddall)

Abellio London often operates rail replacement contracts in the London area, taking the fleet to areas out of the traditional operating area of the company. However, this is not the case here with 9769 (YN51KWD), which is photographed at Ealing Broadway, an area once dominated by First London. Abellio London has since acquired a number of contracts in the area. (Liam Farrer-Beddall)

Nelson's Column at Trafalgar Square can be clearly seen in the background of this photograph of 9775 (KU02YBK). Originally numbered TA75, 9775 is seen travelling down Whitehall on route 3 to Crystal Palace. (Liam Farrer-Beddall)

Twenty-two Alexander ALX400-bodied Dennis Tridents owned by Abellio London were loaned to Stagecoach UK Bus Events for the duration of the London 2012 Olympic Games, all being repainted white. 9786 (KV02USB) is seen exiting the Eaton Manor Transport Hub. This photograph gives a snapshot of the variety used on the contracts. On the left is an Enviro 400 of Travel West Midlands, a similar vehicle owned by Stagecoach. Behind 9786 the rear of an Ulsterbus Volvo B9TL can be seen, while the roof of a Stagecoach Enviro 300 can be seen to the right of the Trident. (Liam Farrer-Beddall)

Abellio London's 9794 (KV02USL) is seen negotiating the roadworks at Victoria while heading towards Waterloo station on route 211. (Liam Farrer-Beddall)

Since route 343 was won by Travel London it had been traditionally operated by Wright Eclipse Gemini-bodied Volvo B7TLs. However, Peckham town centre finds 9812 (LG52HWN) operating the service, heading towards New Cross Gate. (Liam Farrer-Beddall)

Another view of the parking ground behind Clapham Junction station. In this view we see 9820 (LG52XYN) on layover, before heading back to Earl's Court on route C3. (Liam Farrer-Beddall)

Fourteen ALX400s were acquired from Dawson Rentals in February 2011, having previously operated with Armchair and Metroline. They were purchased for the 172 (St Pauls–Brockley Rise), and allocated to Walworth garage. 9832 (KN52NDD) is seen heading to the latter destination, about to cross Waterloo Bridge. (Liam Farrer-Beddall)

Golden Tours first appeared on the London sightseeing tour scene in 2011. V138MEV arrived with the company in March 2011 from Ensign Bus, after being sold by Stagecoach London. It was new to this company in November 1999. It is seen passing through Marble Arch in partial open-top layout. (Liam Farrer-Beddall)

In addition to London sightseeing work, Golden Tours also operated a tourist service to the Harry Potter Studio Tour at the Warner Brothers Studios in Leavesden, Watford. For this they originally used a couple of Alexander ALX400-bodied Dennis Tridents. 168 (V168MEV) shows off the original livery worn by the vehicles, as it leaves Victoria for its journey north. (Liam Farrer-Beddall)

Another view of V362OWC, a former Stagecoach London Trident acquired by Golden Tours. It entered the fleet in May 2011, gaining fleet number 362. It lasted with Golden Tours until June 2016 when it was sold. Victoria Embankment provides the location of this photograph. (Liam Farrer-Beddall)

Ten former Stagecoach London Transbus Tridents with ALX400 bodywork were taken on long-term loan by Tower Transit at Westbourne Park garage. They were predominantly used on the 23 (Liverpool Street Station–Ladbroke Grove). TAL33204 (LX04FXW), formerly Stagecoach London's 18231, is seen heading towards Ladbroke Grove, passing through Marble Arch. (Liam Farrer-Beddall)

LX03BTV was a slightly older model hired from Ensign Bus. Formerly numbered 17753 with Stagecoach London, it was given rolling stock number TAL33208 for the duration of its stay with Tower Transit. It is seen at Trafalgar Square while heading towards Liverpool Street. (Liam Farrer-Beddall)

London City Tours purchased a number of former London Transbus ALX400-bodied Tridents from Dawson Rentals that were new to Armchair, Brentford for the 237. KN52NDE was one such vehicle, acquired by the company during September 2017, and was converted to partial open-top layout. It lasted less than a year, after which London City Tours closed down. KN52NDE is now operating for a tour operator in Dublin. (Liam Farrer-Beddall)

KN52NCE is another former Armchair, Brentford Transbus Trident/ALX400. It was acquired by London City Tours in June 2017, and like KN52NDE, it too passed to a tour operator in Dublin in 2019. This example was built to full open-top layout. (Liam Farrer-Beddall)

Volvo was the last to introduce a chassis on the Alexander ALX400, the B7TL model first being introduced in 1999 on the Plaxton President model. Go-Ahead London's London Central operation was the first London operator to use the B7TL in service, taking forty-five of the type in early 2000. AVL1 (V101LGC) preceded the delivery of these, arriving at Camberwell in December 1999, and entering service on route 45. It is seen here on layover while operating a rail replacement service. (David Beddall)

AVL35 (V135LGC) was one of twenty-seven AVLs allocated to Peckham garage and mostly used on the 63. An influx of Enviro 400s at Peckham led to the transfer of a number of AVLs to Camberwell. The parking ground at the rear of the Camberwell garage is the location of this photograph. (David Beddall)

London United was the next London operator to take stock of the Volvo B7TL/Alexander ALX400 combination. The first batch of twenty-six arrived in February 2000 and were allocated to Shepherds Bush garage for route 220. VA63 (V179OOE) is captured by the camera passing through Twickenham town centre while heading towards Tolworth on route 281. (Liam Farrer-Beddall)

Shepherds Bush garage provides the backdrop to this photograph of VA71 (V187OOE), seen at rest blinded for the 220. The centre staircase fitted to the original batch of Alexander ALX400s can be clearly seen in this view. (David Beddall)

A number of London Buses are retained by their owners after they become life expired on Transport for London contracts. A number of them become driver training vehicles, as has been demonstrated on a number of occasions in this book. Others were added to the private hire fleets, which normally gain a different livery to distinguish them from the main fleet. This was what happened to VA81 (V204OOE) in March 2013. In 2016, RATP renumbered its fleet into a five-digit system, VA81 gaining new rolling stock number VA40381. It is seen wearing United Motorcoach livery while attending the Spring 2016 gathering at the London Bus Museum in Brooklands, Surrey. (Liam Farrer-Beddall)

Eighteen further Alexander ALX400-bodied B7TLs were delivered to Hounslow garage in March and April 2000 for routes 111, 120, 337 and H32. VA92 (W126EON) transferred to Shepherds Bush in May 2010, where it joined the earlier batch on the 220. It is photographed rounding Shepherds Bush Green. (Liam Farrer-Beddall)

Hounslow bus station finds Volvo B7TL VA96 (W131EON) between duties on route 81. The vehicle is devoid of any company logos in this view. (David Beddall)

Hounslow garage provides the backdrop for this photograph of VA305 (SK52USC). It is seen wearing the smart distinctive grey, red and white livery of London United. (Liam Farrer-Beddall)

Shepherds Bush received a second batch of B7TLs with ALX400 bodywork between November 2002 and January 2003 for use on the 148. After replacement by newer rolling stock, ten of the batch were retained by London United and transferred to Hounslow for further use, the other nine being sold. VA306 (SK52USD) was one of those transferred in August 2007. It is seen loading at Brunell bus station, Slough for its return journey to Hounslow. (Liam Farrer-Beddall)

Twenty-eight B7TLs were purchased by First London, arriving in January 2003, and were allocated class code VFL. They were all allocated to Westbourne Park garage and used on route 10 between Kings Cross and Hammersmith. VFL1250 (LT52WVN) is seen passing Marble Arch Underground station bound for Kings Cross. It is followed by a Stagecoach London Trident with similar bodywork. Note the split window on the upper deck of the Trident behind. (David Beddall)

October 2003 saw the renumbering of the First London fleet into a national series that was gradually introduced by First Group. VFL1253 (LT52WVY) became VNL32253 at this time. It is seen on Oxford Street sporting the willow leaf livery worn by the London fleet. (David Beddall)

Arriva London was late to take stock of the Alexander ALX400-bodied Volvo B7TL model, the first arriving in 2003. Fifty-five of the type were taken into stock at Arriva London South's Norwood garage during the summer of 2003, forming a common user pool on double-deck routes from Norwood. One such route was the 2, and it is on this route that we find VLA5 (LJ03MXV) rounding Marble Arch, operating a short working on the 2. (Liam Farrer-Beddall)

Another of the early batch of B7TLs allocated to Norwood is VLA10 (LJ03MYA). It is photographed on Marine Parade, Brighton while operating a private hire job. It is seen sporting the 100 per cent red livery. (Liam Farrer-Beddall)

Brixton finds another of Norwood's allocation of VLAs. VLA12 (LJ03MYC) is seen heading towards its home garage after travelling in from Central London. It is followed by the ALX400's replacement, the Enviro 400. It is seen sporting the 100 per cent red livery. (Liam Farrer-Beddall)

VLA38 (LJ53BBZ) is another of the fifty-five-strong fleet of ALX400-bodied Volvo B7TLs allocated to Norwood garage in September 2003. It is seen wearing 100 per cent red livery at Marble Arch bound for Marylebone on route 2. (Liam Farrer-Beddall)

2014 was designated as the year of the bus by Transport for London, a logo for this being displayed on the side of VLA47 (LJ53BAO). It is seen paused at Victoria Underground station bound for Marylebone. (Liam Farrer-Beddall)

2004 saw fourteen Volvo B7TLs delivered to Arriva The Original London Sightseeing Tour for route 337 (Richmond–Clapham Junction). DWs from Brixton covered for the late arrival of these vehicles. VLA56 is seen on layover at Richmond bus station. (Liam Farrer-Beddall)

Another view taken at Richmond bus station, this time of VLA68 (LJ04YWX). The 337 batch of VLAs were originally allocated to Wandsworth garage. After the loss of the 337 in 2011, VLA56-69 transferred to Norwood for further use. (Liam Farrer-Beddall)

Thirty VLA class ALX400s were delivered to Tottenham garage and put to use on the 123 (Wood Green–Ilford). VLA82 (LJ54BFM) represents the batch, starting its journey to Wood Green, in Ilford town centre. It shows the original livery worn by these vehicles. (Liam Farrer-Beddall)

VLA92 (LJ54BDX) is another of the thirty ALX400-bodied B7TLs allocated to Tottenham for the 123. It is seen off route, operating a journey on the 41 towards Tottenham Hale at Turnpike Lane. (Liam Farrer-Beddall)

Turnpike Lane station provides the backdrop for this photograph of VLA103 (LJ54BCV), seen heading towards Ilford sporting the 100 per cent red livery. The batch allocated to the 123 were shorter than previous deliveries, measuring 10.1 metres in length, the previous VLAs being 10.6 metres in length. (Liam Farrer-Beddall)

Twenty-five VLA class B7TLs were taken into stock in March and April 2005 for Norwood garage. However, the late arrival of DW class buses to cover the conversion of route 19 to low-floor buses saw this batch initially allocated to Brixton. They were soon transferred to their intended garage, where they remained until transfer to other garages between 2010 and 2013. During 2016, a number of these vehicles were allocated to the former Arriva Southern Counties garage at Grays, where they were used for TfL work. VLA106 (LJ05BLF) is seen operating the traditionally single-deck route 66 (Romford Station–Leytonstone), parked on layover at the latter terminus. (Liam Farrer-Beddall)

Barking gained its first allocation of Volvo B7TLs in the summer of 2005, when fifteen ALX400-bodied examples were taken into stock to operate route 128. In 2017, TfL took the decision to route-brand services passing through the Barkingside area of East London, the 128 being one of those routes. Purple was the chosen colour, the branding applied being demonstrated by VLA134 (LJ05GPZ). It is captured by the camera at Romford station. (Liam Farrer-Beddall)

Sister vehicle VLA135 (LJ05GRF) is seen operating the route shortly after delivery to Arriva. It is seen heading for the bus park behind Romford station. The shift from the central staircase shown in the picture of AVL1 earlier in this book can be compared to the location of the staircase on this model. (Liam Farrer-Beddall)

VLA147 (LJ55BTX) is seen having just passed through Trafalgar Square heading for Paddington Basin on route 159. VLA147 formed part of the batch of ALX400-bodied Volvo B7TLs that replaced the last of the AEC Routemasters from mainstream London service. (Liam Farrer-Beddall)

The final thirty-six VLAs arrived at Brixton in November and December 2005 to replace Routemasters on the 159, the last Routemaster service in London, with the exception of the heritage routes 9 and 15. VLA166 (LJ55BVU) is seen at Trafalgar Square heading towards Streatham, followed by a Mercedes-Benz Citaro G bendybus on the 453. (Liam Farrer-Beddall)

Another of the 159 batch, VLA173 (LJ55BVE), is seen travelling down Haymarket bound for Streatham Hill. Like the batch purchased for the 128, the thirty-six taken into stock for the 159 also measured 10.1 metres in length. (David Beddall)

In April 2012, thirteen VLAs were transferred to Arriva Southern Counties at Grays for further use on Transport for London work. Former VLA120 (LJ05BKO) is seen departing Lakeside Shopping Centre's bus station bound for Romford Market on the 370. Upon transfer VLA120 became 6120 in the Arriva Southern Counties fleet. A reorganisation of Arriva's operations in London and the Home Counties saw Grays garage transfer to the control of Arriva London, along with Dartford and Garston, with 6120 regaining its old fleet number. (Liam Farrer-Beddall)

Arriva The Shires & Essex received a slightly larger batch of sixteen Volvo B7TLs from Arriva London during October 2012, and were allocated to route 142 (Watford Junction–Brent Cross). 6176 (LJ55BVH) is seen about to enter Edgware station, with the front end of 6164 visible. (Liam Farrer-Beddall)

The batch of former VLAs also saw service on the 340 (Edgware–Harrow). 6179 (LJ55BVM) is again captured entering Edgware station, having completed a journey on the 340 from Harrow. It is followed by an Enviro 200 owned by London Sovereign, which has travelled in from Arnos Grove on the 251. (Liam Farrer-Beddall)

Acknowledgements

First and foremost, a big thank you goes to my wife Helen who always supports me with my projects for Amberley. Another big thank you goes to my nephew Liam Farrer-Beddall, who always allows me full access to his photo collection, and takes the time to read through my drafts. To Aethan Blake for putting his photo collection at my disposal, and for taking time to proofread some of the captions. Lastly, to Gary Seamarks and Ian Armstrong for providing additional images for this book.

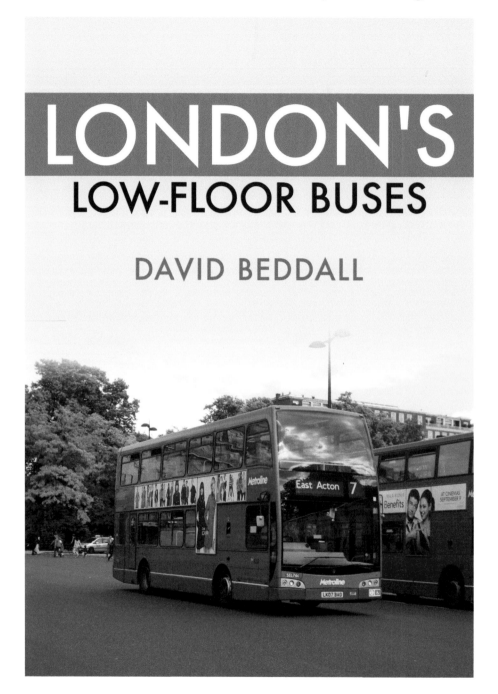